EXTREME LABYRINTHS
CITYSCAPES

Thomas Radclyffe

THUNDER BAY
P·R·E·S·S

San Diego, California

HOW TO USE

Welcome to this book of mesmerizing mazes. The pages ahead contain pathways that take you on a journey through a range of abstract cityscapes. Work your way from the red square at the start, and aim to finish at the red circle. If you get really stuck along the way, you could always allow yourself a glance at the solutions at the back of the book.

START   FINISH

INTRODUCTION

One of the most enjoyable aspects of creating my artwork is watching how people interact with the images. Perhaps because of our everyday experiences with urban landscapes, I found that people were naturally drawn to looking for paths and connections in my cities. The transition to a maze seemed a natural progression—giving a defined route for you to look for while controlling how you navigate the space. I really liked the idea of fusing mazes with my images to create a book that can be enjoyed as both artwork and puzzle.

I started drawing buildings seriously in the second year of my BA. My first brief was to explore Winchester Cathedral with a series of drawings exploring pattern and color. From there I developed my images into more abstract architectural textures. For a long time I drew existing buildings, drawing from life or images online, but I soon wanted to explore my ability to create my own worlds and produce images without reference.

Now, my work is almost always imaginary, focusing on intricate, abstracted cityscapes. I like to create images that have elements of spontaneity, starting with a simple wire-frame outline and constructing the landscape one building at a time. The drawn world follows different rules and I am able to layer building upon building, cramming architecture together to make impossible walkways and twisted perspectives. I see each drawing as a part of a whole; small districts within a continually expanding city.

My inspiration comes from multiple origins. Artists such as Piranesi, Ferriss, and Escher are serious influences, as well as authors like Calvino and Borges. I like taking an idea and playing with how I translate it into an image, often exploding the scale or the quantity; one bridge becomes a city of bridges, or a decorative window is transformed into a giant triumphal arch. Because I don't plan my drawings, the outcome is often unexpected, and happy accidents create neat relationships between buildings, like paths that meet, or harsh juxtapositions. The element of surprise is always exciting.

I have really enjoyed the process of making this book. It has been a great experience both exploring new cityscapes and revisiting some I had forgotten. I hope you enjoy completing these mazes as much as I did creating them. Try not to get lost!

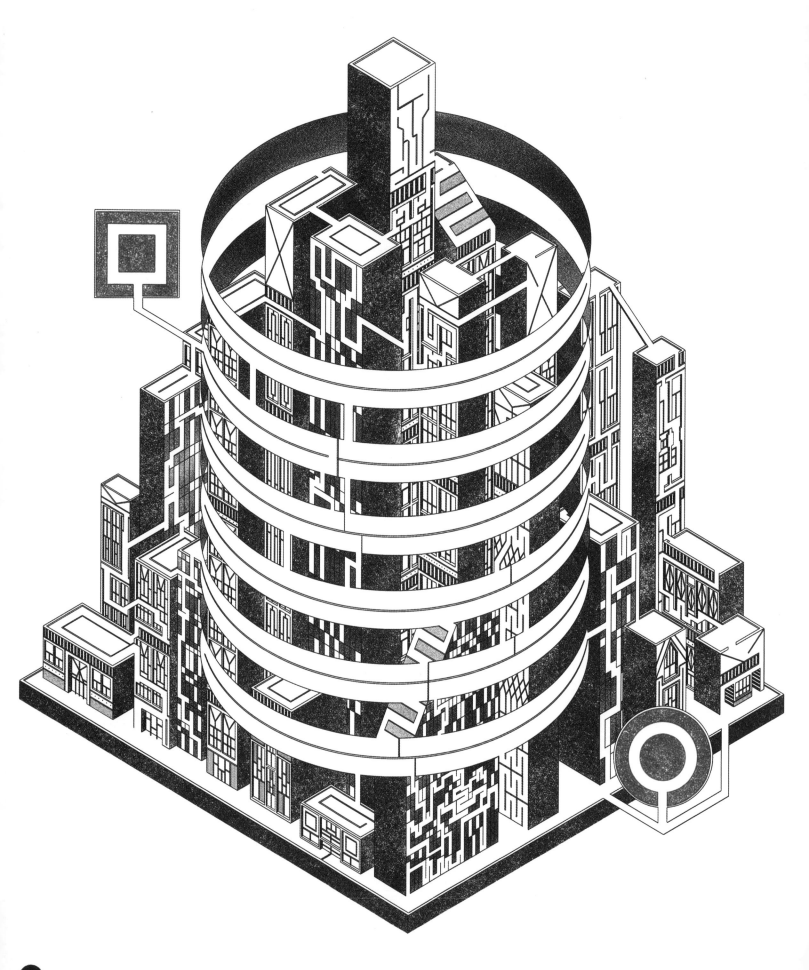

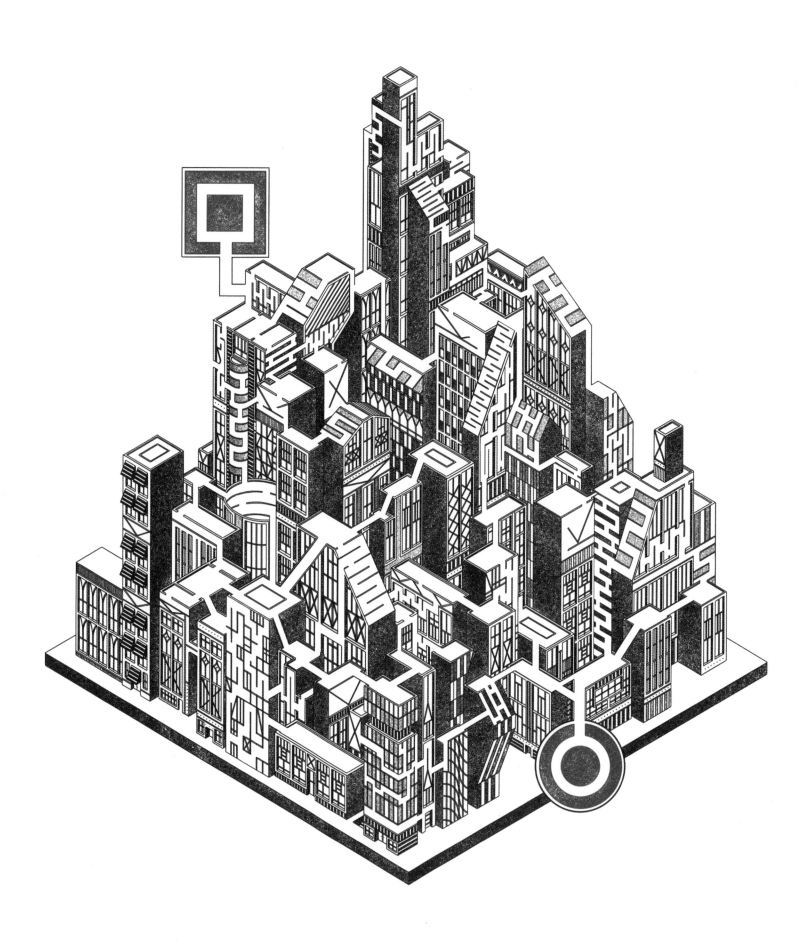

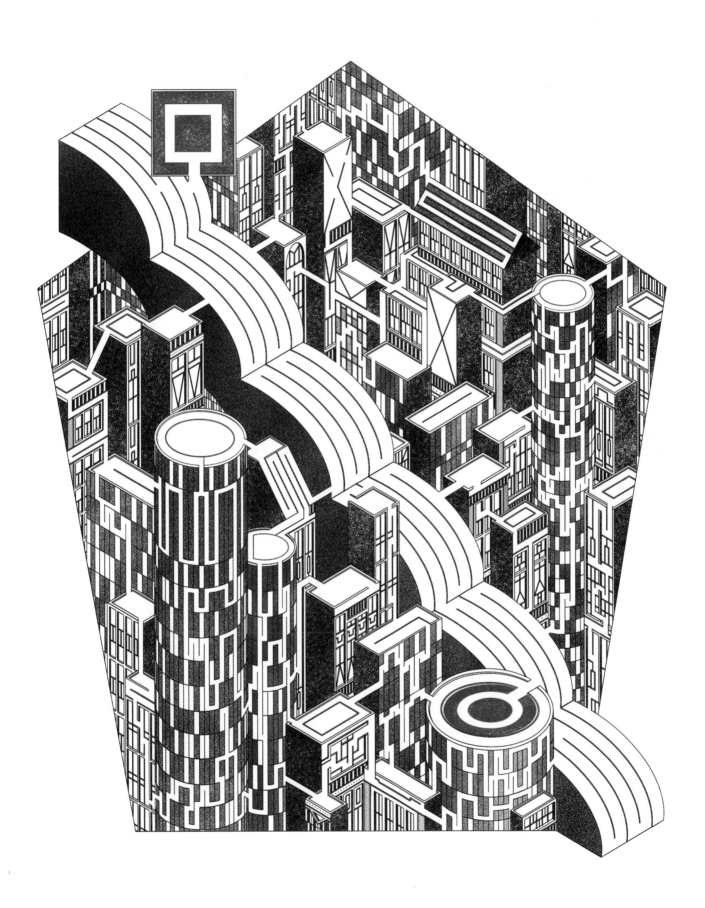

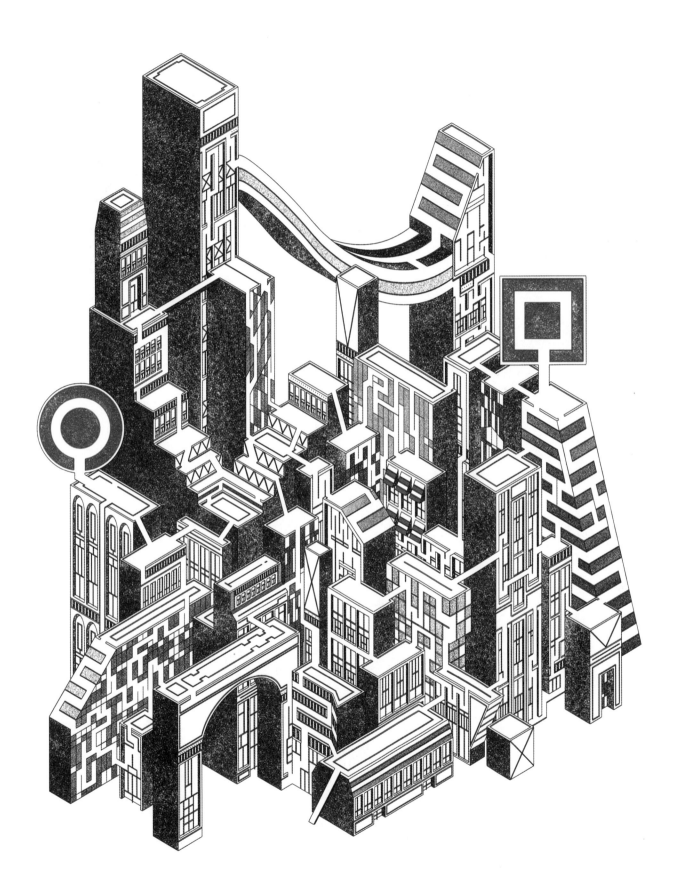

45

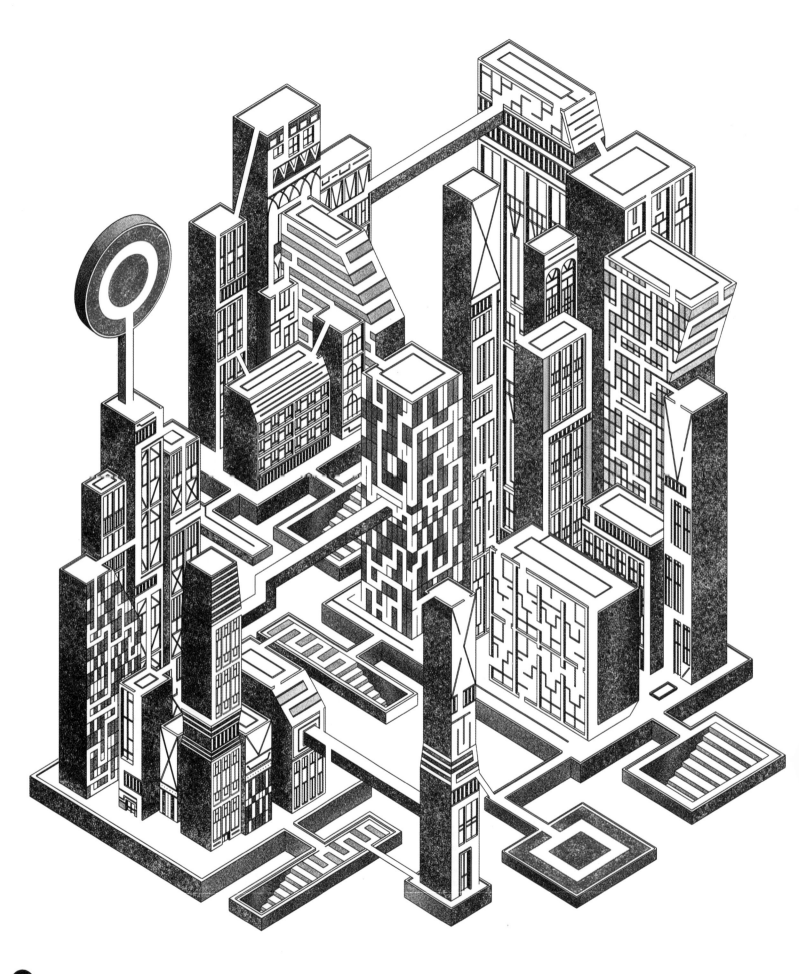

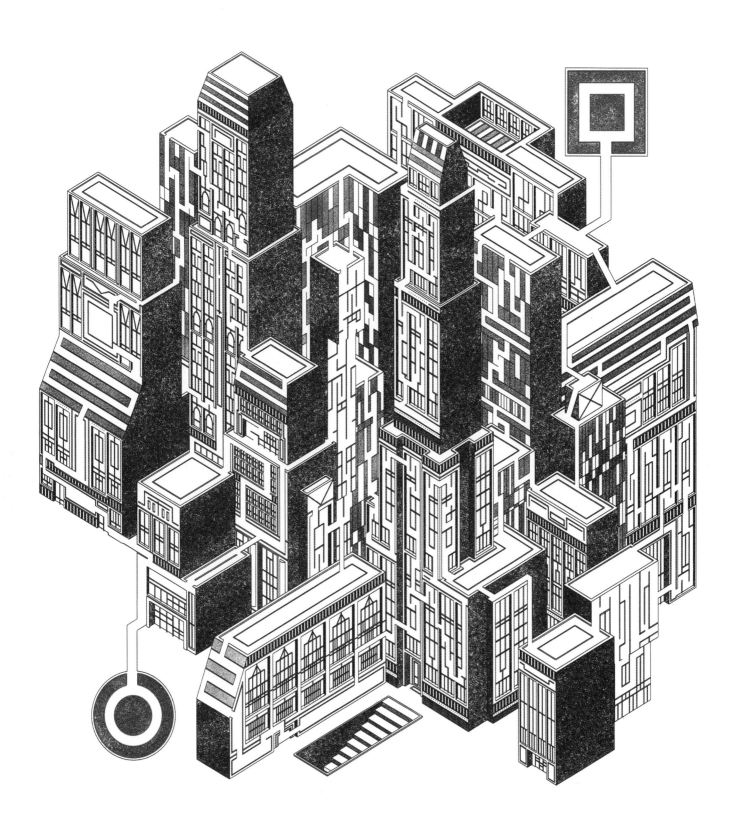

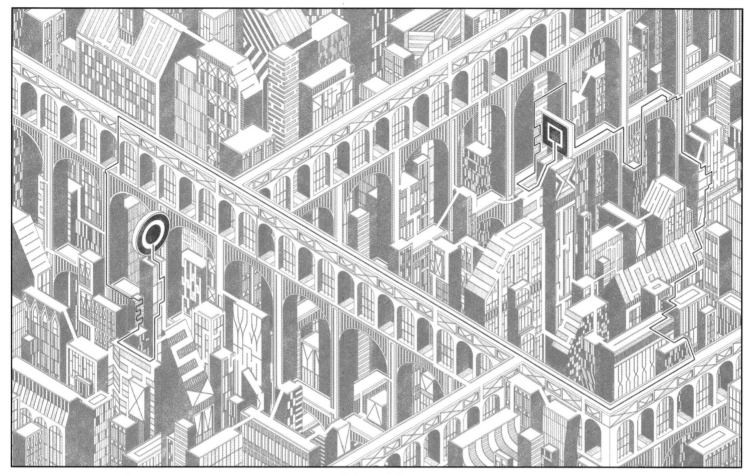

Pages 4–5

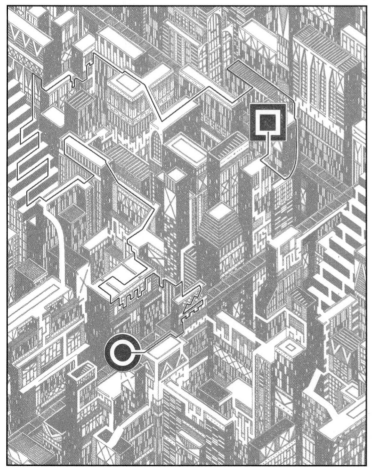

Page 6

Page 7

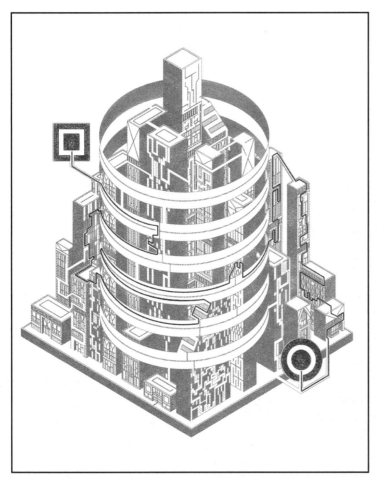

Page 8

Page 9

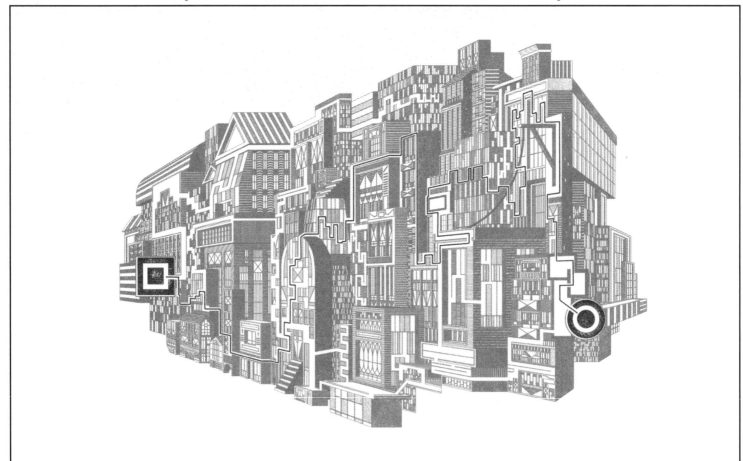

Pages 10–11

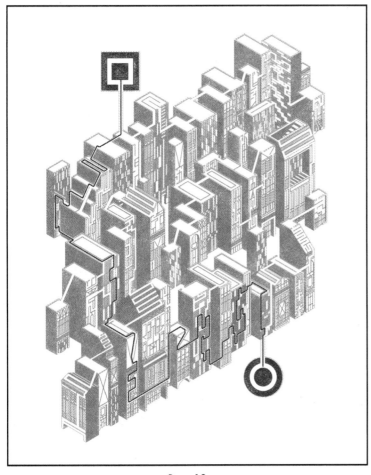

Page 12

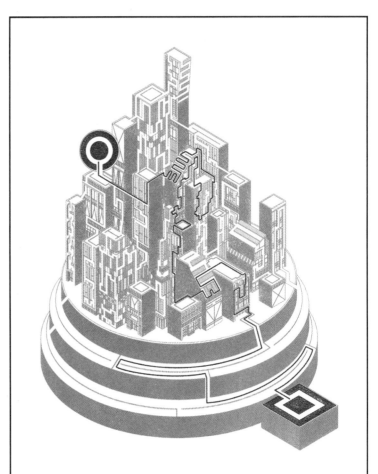

Page 13

Page 14

Page 15

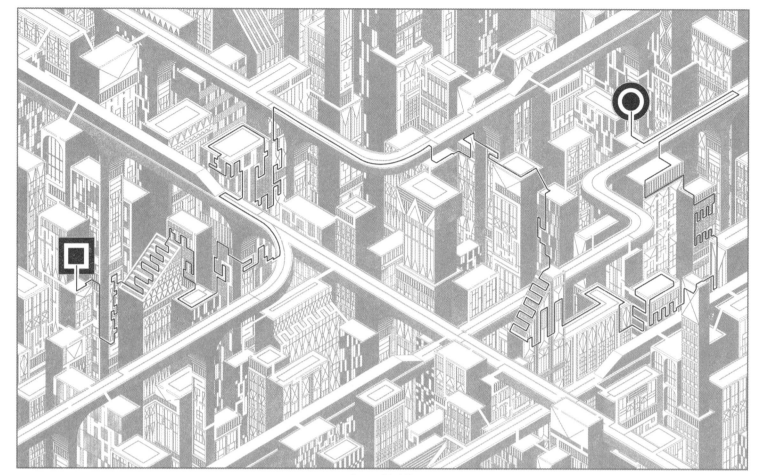

Pages 16–17

Page 18

Page 19

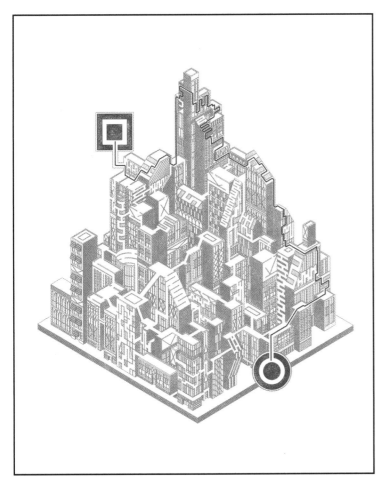

Page 20

Page 21

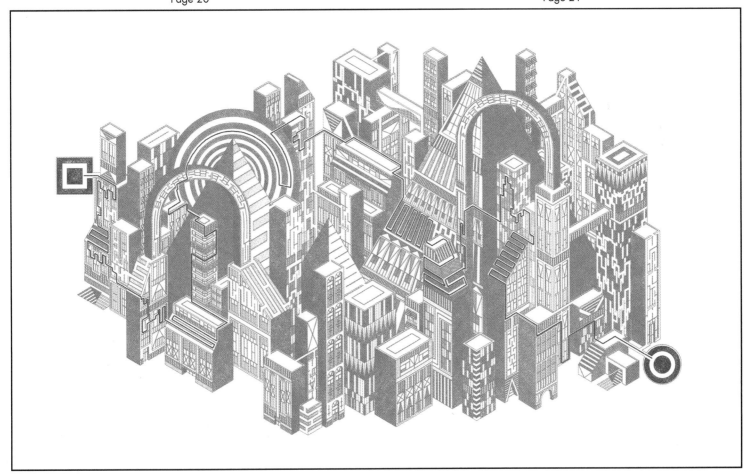

Pages 22–23

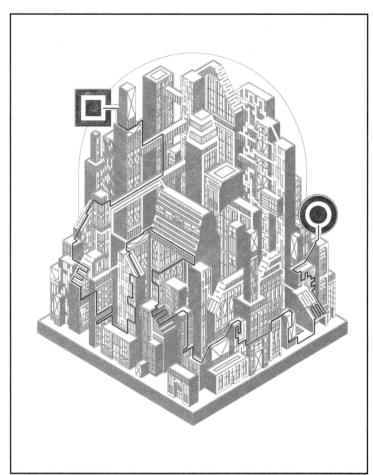

Page 24

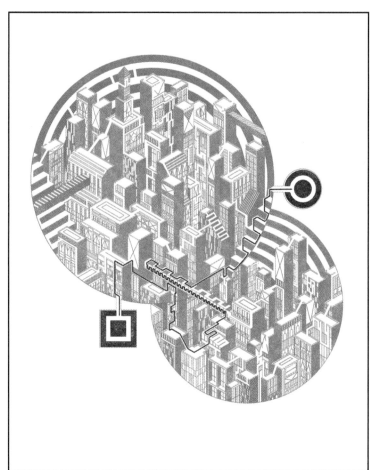

Page 25

Page 26

Page 27

Pages 28–29

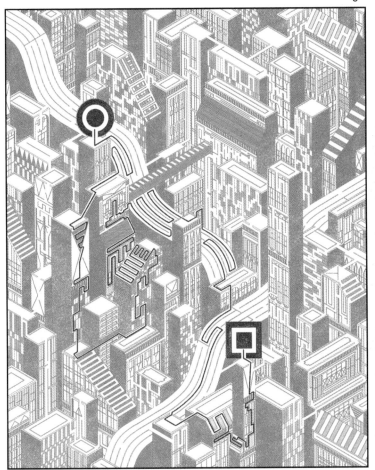

Page 30

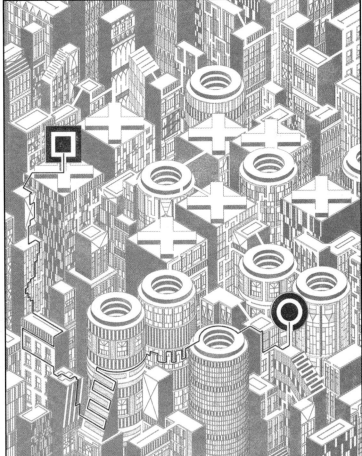

Page 31

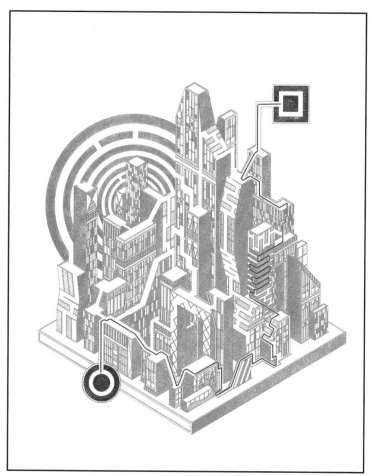

Page 32

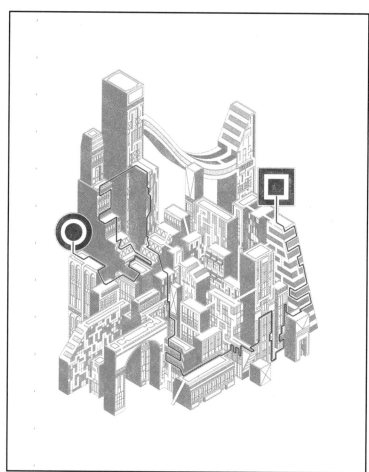

Page 33

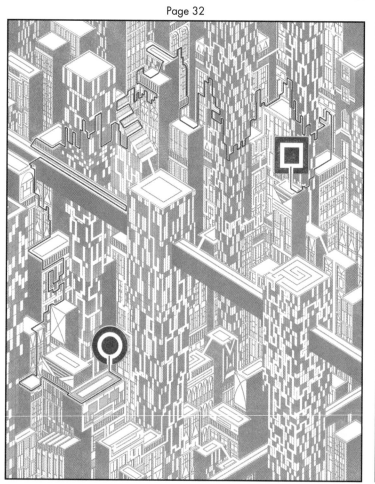

Page 34

Page 35

Pages 36–37

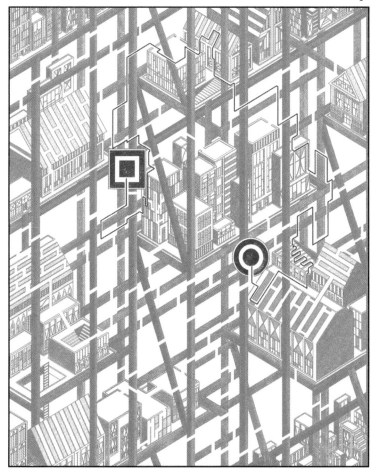

Page 38

Page 39

Page 40

Page 41

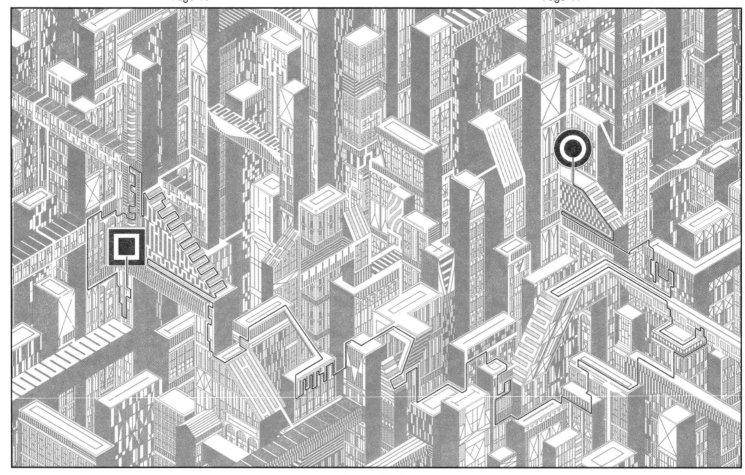

Pages 42–43

Page 44

Page 45

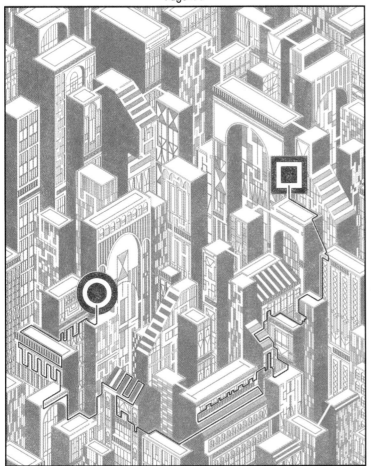

Page 46

Page 47

Pages 48–49

Page 50

Page 51

Page 52

Page 53

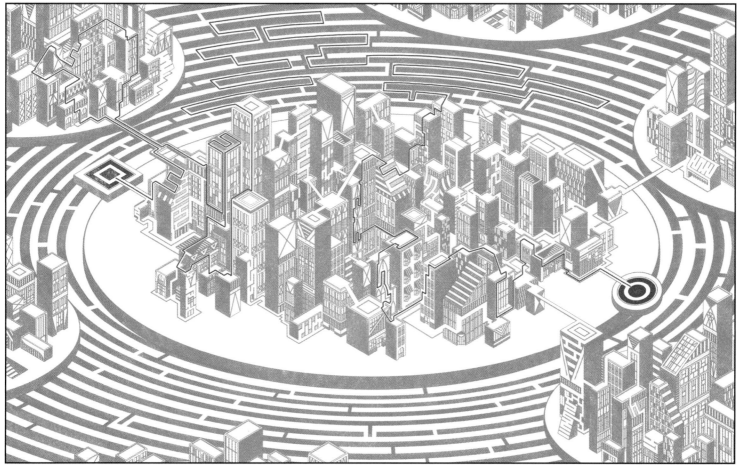

Pages 54–55

Page 56

Page 57

Page 58

Page 59

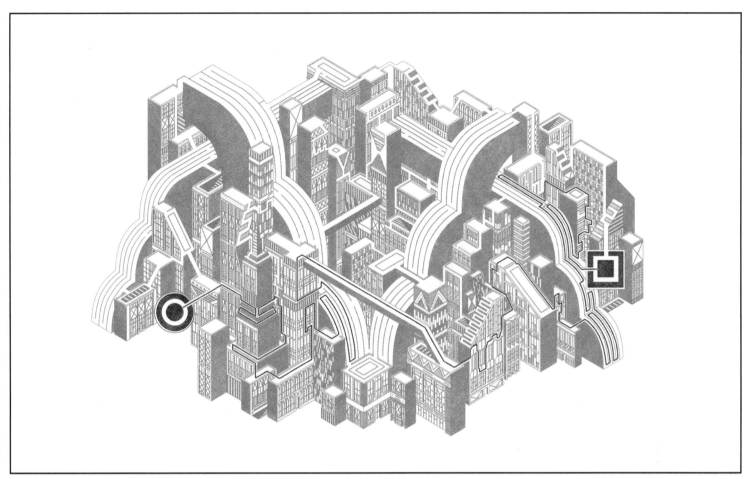

Pages 60–61

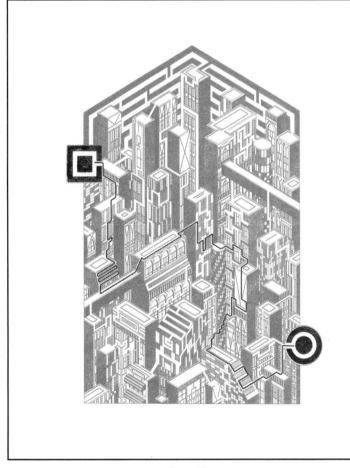

Page 62

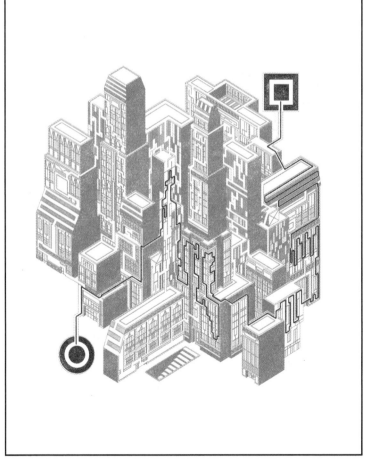

Page 63

Thunder Bay Press
An imprint of Printers Row Publishing Group
10350 Barnes Canyon Road, Suite 100, San Diego, CA 92121
www.thunderbaybooks.com

Printers Row Publishing Group is a division of Readerlink Distribution Services, LLC.
Thunder Bay Press is a registered trademark of Readerlink Distribution Services, LLC.

All notations of errors or omissions should be addressed to Thunder Bay Press, Editorial
Department, at the above address. All other correspondence (author inquiries,
permissions) concerning the content of this book should be addressed to Carlton Books
Ltd, 20 Mortimer Street, London, W1T 3JW, United Kingdom.

Carlton Books Ltd
Editorial Manager: Chris Mitchell
Design Manager: Luke Griffin
Production: Jessica Arvidsson

Thunder Bay Press
Publisher: Peter Norton
Associate Publisher: Ana Parker
Publishing/Editorial Team: April Farr, Kelly Larsen, Kathryn C. Dalby
Editorial Team: JoAnn Padgett, Melinda Allman, Dan Mansfield

ISBN: 978-1-68412-785-6

Printed in Dubai

23 22 21 20 19 1 2 3 4 5